A TRUE BOOK™

Women's History in the U.S.

WOMEN in the Old West

Marti Dumas

Children's Press®
An Imprint of Scholastic Inc.

Content Consultant
Holly Hynson, MA
Department of History
University of Maryland, College Park

Thank you to Elise McMullen-Ciotti for her insights into Indigenous Peoples' history and culture.

A CIP catalog record of this book is available from the Library of Congress.
ISBN 978-0-531-13080-3 (library binding) 978-0-531-13339-2 (paperback)

Scholastic Inc., 557 Broadway, New York, NY 10012

1 2 3 4 5 6 7 8 9 10 R 30 29 28 27 26 25 24 23 22 21

Book produced by 22 MEDIAWORKS, INC.
Book design by Amelia Leon / Fabia Wargin Design

Front cover: A trick rider in a Wild West show.
Back cover: Settlers camp along the trail.

Find the Truth

Everything you are about to read is true *except* for one of the sentences on this page.

Which one is **TRUE**?

T or F   Women were allowed to own land in the Old West.

T or F   Married women were allowed to work as teachers in the Old West.

Find the answers in this book.

Contents

Indigenous people harvesting rice

The **BIG** Truth

Destroying Indigenous Peoples' Ways of Life

Women voting in Wyoming

3 Power in the Law

What freedoms did women have in the Old West?

May Manning Lillie

4 Women and the Myth of the Old West

How did women help create the myth of the "Wild West"?

5

A Crossing of Cultures

What we call **"The Old West" began around 1850,** as **settlers** living in crowded eastern and southern parts of the United States **began to migrate west** of the Mississippi River. At that time, **the United States claimed the land that exists within its borders today,** but much of it was unsettled **territories that had not yet been divided into states.**

Wagon trains included hundreds of people. There was safety in numbers.

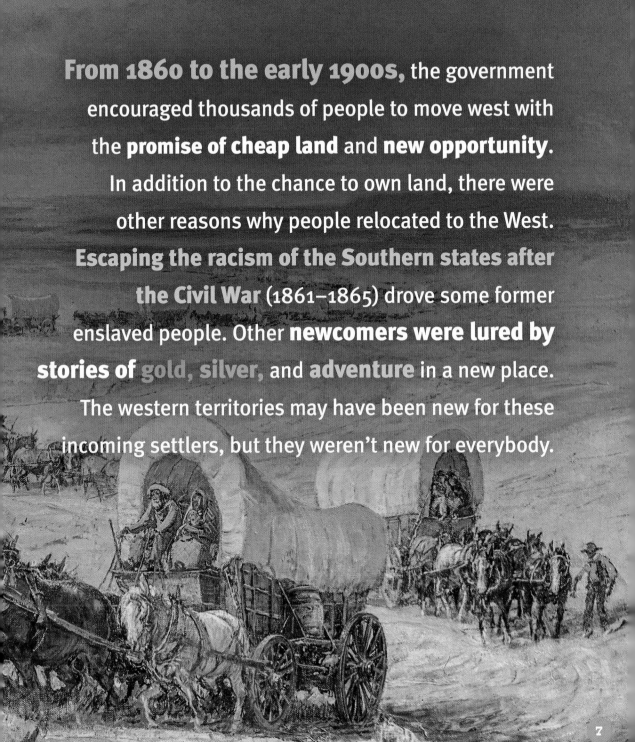

From 1860 to the early 1900s, the government encouraged thousands of people to move west with the **promise of cheap land** and **new opportunity**. In addition to the chance to own land, there were other reasons why people relocated to the West. **Escaping the racism of the Southern states after the Civil War** (1861–1865) drove some former enslaved people. Other **newcomers were lured by stories of** gold, silver, and **adventure** in a new place. The western territories may have been new for these incoming settlers, but they weren't new for everybody.

At the time, **land west of the Mississippi was already the home of numerous Native Nations** who had lived there for thousands of years. **Other nations had been moved there in the 1830s** when the U.S. government forced those in the east **to migrate on foot to western territories,** giving settlers more room. **Those forced migrations are often called a "Trail of Tears,"** by Indigenous people.

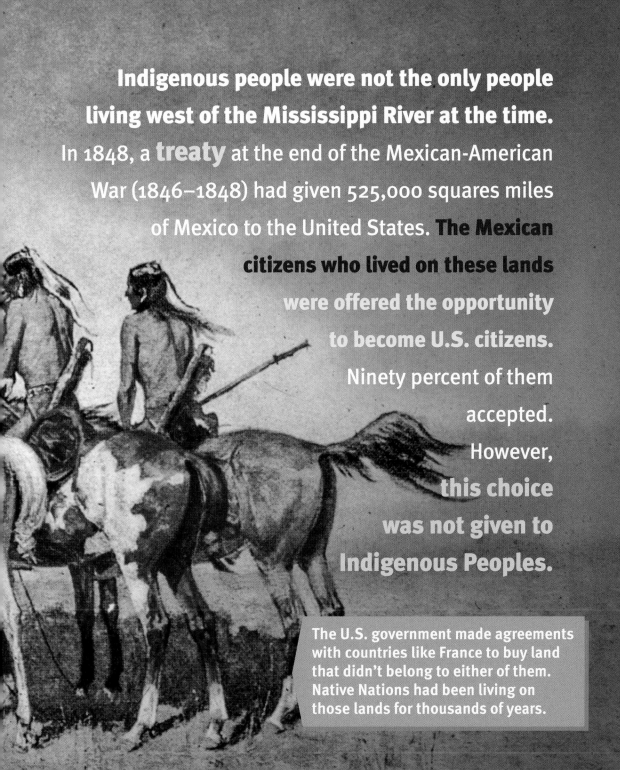

Indigenous people were not the only people living west of the Mississippi River at the time. In 1848, a **treaty** at the end of the Mexican-American War (1846–1848) had given 525,000 squares miles of Mexico to the United States. **The Mexican citizens who lived on these lands were offered the opportunity to become U.S. citizens. Ninety percent of them accepted. However, this choice was not given to Indigenous Peoples.**

The U.S. government made agreements with countries like France to buy land that didn't belong to either of them. Native Nations had been living on those lands for thousands of years.

From 1865 to 1910, vast numbers of new settlers soon arrived in the West, leaving Indigenous people with limited authority and protection. **Among the new arrivals were diverse groups of girls and women,** boys and men, of **European, Asian,** and **African** descent. They brought their own cultures and dreams for a new life.

As these newcomers formed communities, they **created laws that were not always kind or fair to everyone.** They did not protect Asian or Indigenous people, and some laws, like the Chinese Exclusion Act, even **discriminated** against them.

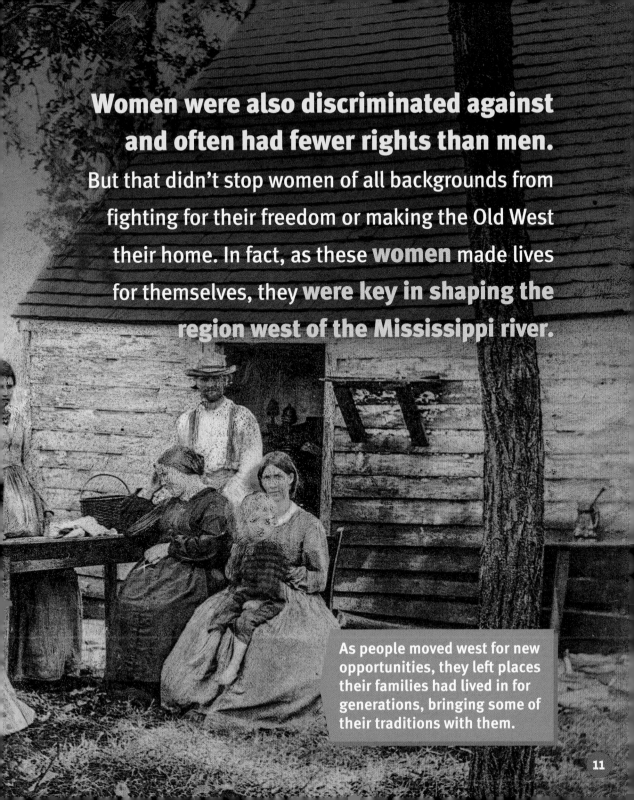

Women were also discriminated against and often had fewer rights than men. But that didn't stop women of all backgrounds from fighting for their freedom or making the Old West their home. In fact, as these women made lives for themselves, they were key in shaping the region west of the Mississippi river.

As people moved west for new opportunities, they left places their families had lived in for generations, bringing some of their traditions with them.

In the Old West, a trip from Missouri to California took about five months. Today the trip would take only two or three days by car.

In wagon trains, women did a lot of the work needed to camp for the night, such as cooking, cleaning, and caring for children and animals.

Heading West

One of the earliest **wagon trains** set out from Elm Grove, Missouri, in 1842. More than 100 settlers traveled in this caravan along the Oregon Trail, a route fur traders and explorers had mapped out in the preceding years. Covered wagons were pulled by oxen, and hundreds of horses, mules, and cattle walked alongside. Settlers traveled through the flat Great Plains, across raging rivers, up the steep mountains of the Rockies, and into lush valleys on their way to Oregon, Utah, or California.

Settlers heading west made fires along the trail at night for cooking and warmth.

People traveling west brought as many things with them as they could. Those who could afford to ride in covered wagons filled them with furniture, food, and other supplies. Other settlers, including enslaved people, walked behind the wagons and had to carry their belongings. This could be dangerous. They risked being run over by wagon wheels, trampled by animals, or simply overcome by exhaustion.

New Opportunities

Settlers traveled during the day, then set up camp to sleep outside at night. Women were usually in charge of cooking and cleaning, but there were some exceptions. Fanny Brooks, for example, joined a wagon train from Nebraska to California with her husband in 1854. Along the long journey, Fanny helped **drive** the mules. Ordinarily, that was considered men's work. But on the journey west there were opportunities for women to take on different roles.

By 1869, some 400,000 people had migrated west along the Oregon Trail.

Fanny Brooks with two of her children

West without Choice

Bridget "Biddy" Mason was an enslaved woman who, in 1851, was forced by her enslaver, Robert Marion Smith, to walk west. She traveled 1,700 miles from Mississippi to settle in the area that would become Salt Lake City, Utah. Mason had to set up camp, tend the cattle, and cook meals. In addition, Mason also looked after pregnant women and took care of her three young children.

By the end of her life, Bridget "Biddy" Mason was a wealthy and influential member of her community. She is credited with founding the First African Methodist Episcopal Church in Los Angeles, California.

Free Black men from the East migrated west in hopes of finding gold during the California gold rush. Some enslaved Black people were forced to mine gold for their owners.

In 1851, Mason's enslaver forced her to walk west again, this time from Utah to California. However, slavery was not legal in California. Free Black people she met along the way encouraged her to challenge her enslaver. Once she reached California, Mason took Robert Marion Smith to court. In 1856 she won her freedom!

Carrie Strahorn and her husband, Robert Strahorn

Some people call Carrie Strahorn "the Mother of the West" because of all the articles, books, and pamphlets she wrote about her frontier travel.

The Railroad

Beginning in 1862, the U.S. government supported the creation of railroads that would stretch all the way from the eastern states to California. One of the new railroads was called the Union Pacific. A woman named Carrie Strahorn helped make it famous. From the late 1870s until 1911, Strahorn and her husband wrote about their train travels to the West. Her writing encouraged many people to make the trip themselves.

Safe rail travel brought even more people to the western territories. But as settlement of the Old West transformed the continent, the way of life for the Indigenous Peoples living there was destroyed. The U.S. military funded the killing of all buffaloes to make way for the railroad and to deprive Indigenous people of their main food source. Tribes were forced to relocate for survival. Buffaloes were driven to the edge of extinction and many Indigenous people perished.

Railroad companies advertised "hunting by rail," a sport that allowed passengers to shoot hundreds of buffaloes without even getting off the train.

Life in the Old West could be lonely for people who lived miles apart. They had little time away from the difficult work of settlement.

Evelyn Cameron, a wealthy settler originally from England, took photographs of life in the Old West in the 1890s.

Women's Work

Women who settled the Old West usually did the same kinds of jobs women did in the East and South. In the 1800s, most women were responsible for domestic labor like cooking, cleaning, caring for children, and doing laundry. However, building new communities in the West took a lot of work. Women were needed to also take on jobs that were usually performed by men, like farming, ranching, teaching, or owning businesses.

Classrooms were not usually split by grade. Children of all ages shared the same classroom.

Women as Teachers

Until the 1840s, most of the teachers in the Old West were men. A woman named Catharine Beecher helped

Catharine Beecher

change that. In 1852, she started an organization that encouraged educated white women in the East to become teachers in the West. By 1858, more than 600 women had traveled to the western territories to teach.

Difficult Conditions

Female teachers in the Old West were paid half as much as male teachers even though they faced the same tough conditions. Many schools were just one room with upward of 60 students. Supplies were hard to come by. Teachers had to be creative, sometimes instructing children to read and write by scratching letters into the dirt with sticks. But for many women, the freedom and opportunities they gained in the West were worth the hardships they endured.

Once a woman married, she was not allowed to teach in the Old West.

Teachers sometimes lived in one-room schoolhouses, like this display at a museum in Cody, Wyoming.

Women as Homesteaders

In 1862, the government created the Homestead Act to encourage more people to move to the West. In many parts of the country, women were not allowed to own land. But the Homestead Act offered land at a low price to anyone who was at least 21 years old and a citizen, including women.

The Homestead Act of 1862 allowed people to buy up to 160 acres of land.

In the Great Plains, where wood was difficult to get, settlers often made houses out of clumps of dirt and grass called sod.

Thanks to the Homestead Act, the land was cheap, but building a homestead could be costly. If homesteaders did not build houses on their land, the government could take it back. In places like the Great Plains, there were few forests, so lumber

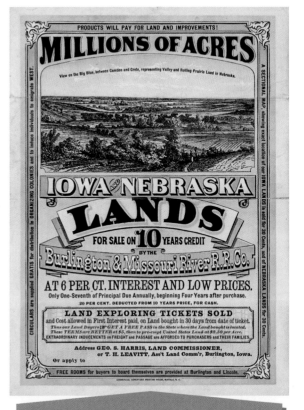

Land companies encouraged people to go west by making it easy to pay for travel and buy supplies.

for building houses was hard to get and therefore expensive. Women who claimed a homestead took on jobs as teachers, laundresses, and nurses to make money for building.

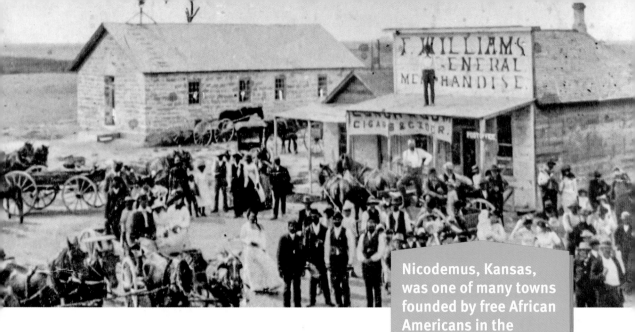

Nicodemus, Kansas, was one of many towns founded by free African Americans in the western territories.

Women of Color

The Homestead Act also made it easier for Black women to move west. After the Civil War, thousands of Black people moved to settlements across the western territories. They hoped to escape the dangerous racism of the South by living in all-Black communities in the West. In 1890, Sarah McCabe and her husband, Edwin, founded Langston City, a community in Oklahoma. By 1891, 200 people lived there, including a doctor, a schoolteacher, and a minister.

Groundbreakers

Mary Fields was the first African American woman to work for the U.S. Postal Service, delivering mail by stagecoach in Montana in the 1890s. A former slave, Mary became an Old West legend. Settler Elizabeth Thorn Scott was a Black woman who had been born free in New York. She moved to California in the 1850s. She opened a school for Black children in Sacramento. Indigenous students and Asian students also attended her school.

Mary Fields

Elizabeth Thorn Scott's daughter, Lydia Flood (pictured), was one of the first students to attend a school open to all races in California in 1872.

The Gold Rush

People hunted for gold and other precious metals in the western territories, including California, Nevada, and Arizona, from the late 1840s all the way through the early 1900s. When a prospector found gold, hundreds of new people would rush to the area, hoping to strike it rich. Most of them didn't. The people who made the most money were the merchants who sold the miners equipment and supplies. Other businesses, including banks, saloons, and hotels, also supported the miners.

In 1850, men take a break from panning for gold. A woman holds a basket that probably has food and other supplies for them.

Nellie Cashman

Many women in the Old West, like Nellie Cashman, started their own businesses. Nellie Cashman was born in Ireland around 1850. She moved to Boston, Massachusetts, when she was a young girl. At the age of 19, she went west to open a business providing supplies for the hundreds of miners looking for gold and silver. Nellie was very successful and eventually settled in Tombstone, Arizona. She used her money to build hospitals, schools, and churches to make her community a better place. She was sometimes known as the "Miner's Angel" and the "Angel of Tombstone."

Destroying Indigenous Peoples' Ways of Life

As settlers moved to the Old West, the U.S. government wanted to bring the Native Nations under its control. This is how the government achieved its goal.

Change the Culture

The cultures of Indigenous people were vastly different from that of the settlers. Government policies dictated that Indigenous people should blend in with the new population of the Old West or become extinct.

Indigenous children, including girls like Zitkála-Ša, a Yankton Sioux girl, were ordered to attend re-education schools. Zitkála-Ša and thousands of other children were separated from their families and forced to learn to read and write in English, change their religions, cut their hair, and wear European-style clothes to make them less "Indian."

Zitkála-Ša

Take the Land

Beginning in the 1830s, the U.S. government forced Indigenous Peoples to move to sections of land, called reserves or reservations, often hundreds of miles away from their original homes. This was done to increase space for white settlers, and so that territories could claim statehood west of Missouri.

Indigenous women worked together to harvest rice.

Exterminate the Buffaloes

In the 1870s, the U.S. military funded the killing of the millions of buffalo grazing the Great Plains. Indigenous people in this region depended on the buffalo herds to live. The herds provided more than just food. Indigenous women also used buffalo for leather, needles, and thread to make everything from shelters to clothes. When the buffaloes were destroyed, so was that way of life.

Many Indigenous people fought these changes and won important victories. For example, women like Buffalo Calf Road Woman and many other Northern Cheyenne fought to protect their land in Montana at the Battle of the Little Bighorn in 1876. However, the Native Nations were eventually devastated by military attacks, massacres, and the introduction of new diseases like small pox in their communities. The damage to their culture and way of life still hurts Indigenous women and girls to this day.

31

Women in Cheyenne, Wyoming, were among the first in the U.S. to get the vote.

Sarah Young was the first woman to vote legally in the United States, on February 14, 1870, in the Utah territory.

CHAPTER

3

Power in the Law

White women and Black women had more **civil rights** in the Old West than they had anywhere else in the country. Wyoming gave anyone who was a citizen the right to vote in 1869. Utah followed, allowing white women the vote in 1870. This was 50 years before the Nineteenth Amendment to the U.S. Constitution, granting women the right to vote, was ratified.

Voting gave women power to support legislators and laws that would improve their lives.

In 1870, Esther Hobart Morris became the first female justice of the peace in the U.S.

According to the census, in 1870 only 10 Black women and five Asian women were qualified to vote in the Wyoming territory.

Women in the Old West took advantage of their political power.

In 1887 Susanna Madora Salter became the first woman in the United States to be elected mayor. She had not planned to run. Her name was put on the **ballot** in Argonia, Kansas, by a group that wanted to embarrass women and discourage them from politics. The prank backfired. Thanks to the large numbers of women who turned out to vote, Susanna Salter won the election with two-thirds of the votes.

Lyda Conley, Wyandot-American Lawyer

In 1902, Lyda Conley became the first Indigenous woman to become a lawyer in the United States. Lyda, who was a member of the Wyandot Nation, used the legal system to protect a Wyandot burying ground in Kansas City. She sued the city to keep it from developing the land. In 1909, she argued her case before the Supreme Court, becoming the first Indigenous person to do so. Although the court did not rule in her favor, Lyda received support from a senator, who proposed a bill that made the cemetery a national park. The bill was passed in 1916.

Lyda Conley and her sisters took turns standing guard with muskets to protect the burial ground.

No Justice for All

Laws in the Old West favored some women. But most Indigenous women were not counted as U.S. citizens, so they could not vote anywhere. Groups that fought for women's suffrage, or the right to vote, often excluded Black women from their organizations. Oregon and parts of California even had laws that made it illegal for Black or Asian people to live there.

Timeline: Women's Civil Rights in the Old West

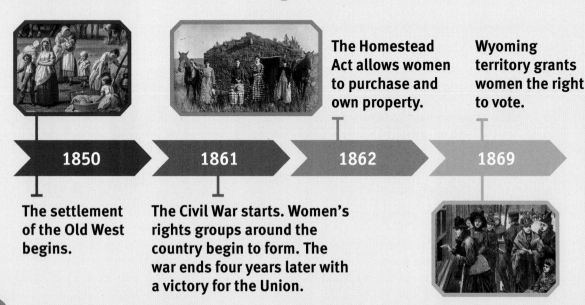

The Homestead Act allows women to purchase and own property.

Wyoming territory grants women the right to vote.

1850   **1861**   **1862**   **1869**

The settlement of the Old West begins.

The Civil War starts. Women's rights groups around the country begin to form. The war ends four years later with a victory for the Union.

Asian women were especially vulnerable in the Old West. Some had traveled to the United States to follow their husbands. Others had been taken there with the promise of a job, but ended up enslaved.

The Old West provided new opportunities for many women, but it would be decades before Indigenous people, Black, or Chinese women were granted equality under the law.

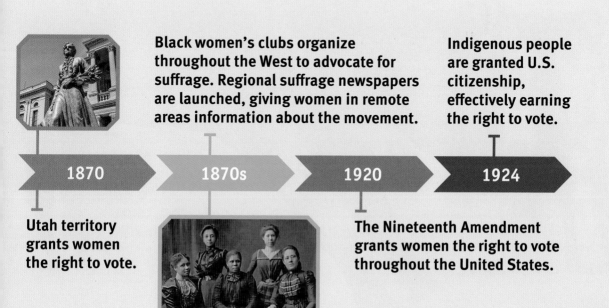

Black women's clubs organize throughout the West to advocate for suffrage. Regional suffrage newspapers are launched, giving women in remote areas information about the movement.

Indigenous people are granted U.S. citizenship, effectively earning the right to vote.

1870   1870s   1920   1924

Utah territory grants women the right to vote.

The Nineteenth Amendment grants women the right to vote throughout the United States.

Women performed in shows like this one, called Cheyenne Frontier Days, to show their skills and entertain the crowds.

★
4

Women and the Myth of the Old West

Stories about the western frontier, like those by Carrie Strahorn, captured people's imaginations. The region was nicknamed the "Wild West" as new communities struggled to create laws and protection for the settlers. Tales of romantic, rugged living spread quickly even in a time before television and the internet—partly because writers and performers were busy selling a western dream.

Annie Oakley became famous performing trick shots in Buffalo Bill's Wild West show.

Wild West Shows

In the 1880s, Wild West shows became popular around the United States and in Europe. The shows made money by depicting what life was like in the "Wild West." The problem was that not everything in the shows was true.

Wild West shows often created stories that made Indigenous people look like villains and white people look like heroes. People all around the world mistook the stories in them for facts.

Women who performed in the shows included sharpshooter Annie Oakley, storyteller Martha Jane Cannary, known as Calamity Jane, and trick rider May Manning Lillie.

Larger-than-life stories of the Old West made their way into books, magazines, and newspapers, but those myths can't trump the true stories of real women. It was the hard work, struggles, joys, and triumphs of thousands of women that shaped the true story of the Old West. ▄

May Manning Lillie

Women Writers of the West

Historians learn a lot from sources that are usually private, like diaries, journals, and letters from women who lived in the Old West. But we can also learn a lot about the Old West from women who were able to make their writing public.

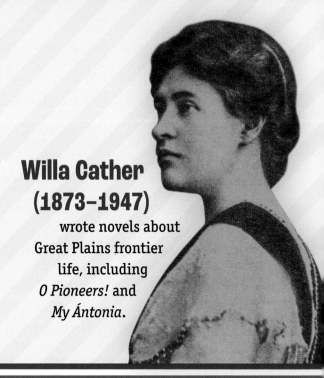

Willa Cather (1873–1947)

wrote novels about Great Plains frontier life, including *O Pioneers!* and *My Ántonia*.

Josie Briggs Hall (1869–1935)

wrote *A Scroll of Facts and Advice*, the first book published by a Black Texan woman.

Helen Hunt Jackson (1830–1885)

was a novelist, poet, and passionate activist who fought for the improved treatment of Indigenous people.

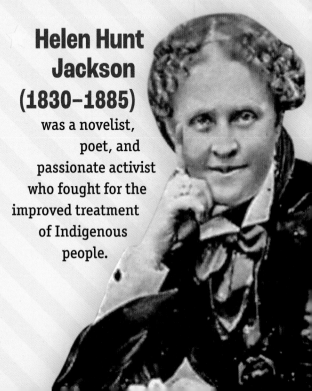

Delilah L. Beasley
(1867–1934)

was a columnist for the *Oakland Tribune* in California in the 1920s and possibly the first African American woman to be published regularly in a major metropolitan newspaper.

Muriel H. Wright
(1889–1975)

was a Choctaw teacher, writer, historian, and editor of *The Chronicles of Oklahoma* who wrote or co-wrote numerous books about the Native Nations of Oklahoma.

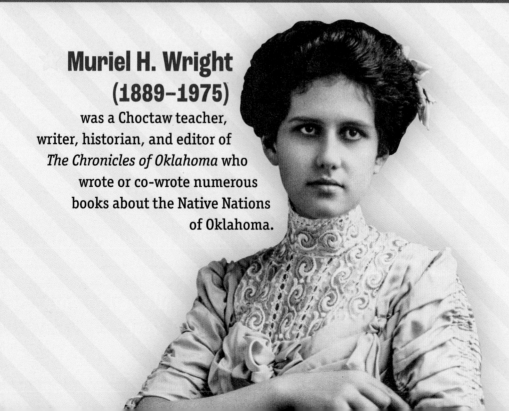

True Statistics

Estimated number of buffaloes that once roamed the Great Plains: 30 to 70 million

Number of acres that the Homestead Act of 1862 granted settlers: Up to 160 acres (65 ha)

Number of miles between Missouri and California: About 2,000 miles (3,200 km)

Number of miles that wagon trains traveled each day: About 10 miles (16 km)

Number of months it took for a wagon train to travel from Missouri to California: More than five months

Length of the first transcontinental railroad running from Omaha, Nebraska, to Sacramento, California: 1,776 miles (2,858 km)

Number of days it took for 36 states to ratify the Nineteenth Amendment granting women the right to vote: 441

Did you find the truth?

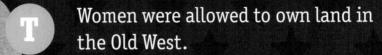

T Women were allowed to own land in the Old West.

F Married women were allowed to work as teachers in the Old West.

Resources

Further Reading

Baym, Nina. *Women Writers of the American West: 1833–1927.* Urbana: University of Illinois Press, 2011.

Bratt, John. *Trails of Yesterday.* Lincoln: University of Nebraska Press, 1996.

Dunbar-Ortiz, Roxanne. *An Indigenous Peoples' History of the United States for Young People.* Boston: Beacon Press, 2019.

Kappler, Charles Joseph. *Indian Affairs: Laws and Treaties.* New York: AMS Press, 1971.

Lindgren, H. Elaine. *Land in Her Own Name: Women as Homesteaders in North Dakota.* Norman: University of Oklahoma Press, 1996.

U.S. National Park Service. "Bridget 'Biddy' Mason." https://www.nps.gov/people/biddymason.htm.

Western Writers of America. *The Women Who Made the West.* Garden City, NY: Doubleday, 1980.

Other Books in the Series

 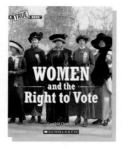 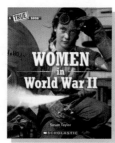 

Glossary

ballot (BAL-uht) a way of voting secretly, using slips of paper or a machine

civil rights (SIV-uhl rytes) the individual rights all members of a democratic society have to freedom and equal treatment under the law

discriminated (dis-KRIM-uh-nay-ted) showed prejudice on the basis of ethnicity, gender, or a similar social factor

drive (drive) to control livestock hitched up to a wagon

settlers (SET-uhl-ers) people who move to a region that has few inhabitants or that is occupied by people of a different ethnic or religious background

territories (TER-i-tor-eez) the land under the control of a state or nation

Trail of Tears (trayl uhv teerz) the route of forced migration taken by Native Nations in North America. The most famous is that of the Creek, Choctaw, Chickasaw, Cherokee, and Seminole Peoples, when the U.S. Army forced them to walk westward over 1,500 miles (2,400 km) from eastern lands to present-day Oklahoma.

treaty (TREE-tee) formal written agreement between two or more nations

wagon trains (WAG-uhn traynz) in frontier times, lines or groups of covered wagons that traveled together for safety

Index

Page numbers in **bold** indicate illustrations.

About the Author

Marti Dumas has a bachelor's degree in women's and gender studies from Amherst College and master's degree in curriculum design and teaching practices from Columbia University Teachers College. Certified to teach Pre-K–12 in Florida and Louisiana, Marti was a classroom teacher for 10 years and functioned as a literacy specialist and lead teacher in both states. She is also the author of several books for children, including *Jaden Toussaint, the Greatest* and the *Seeds of Magic* series.